A-Z JESUS LOVES ME

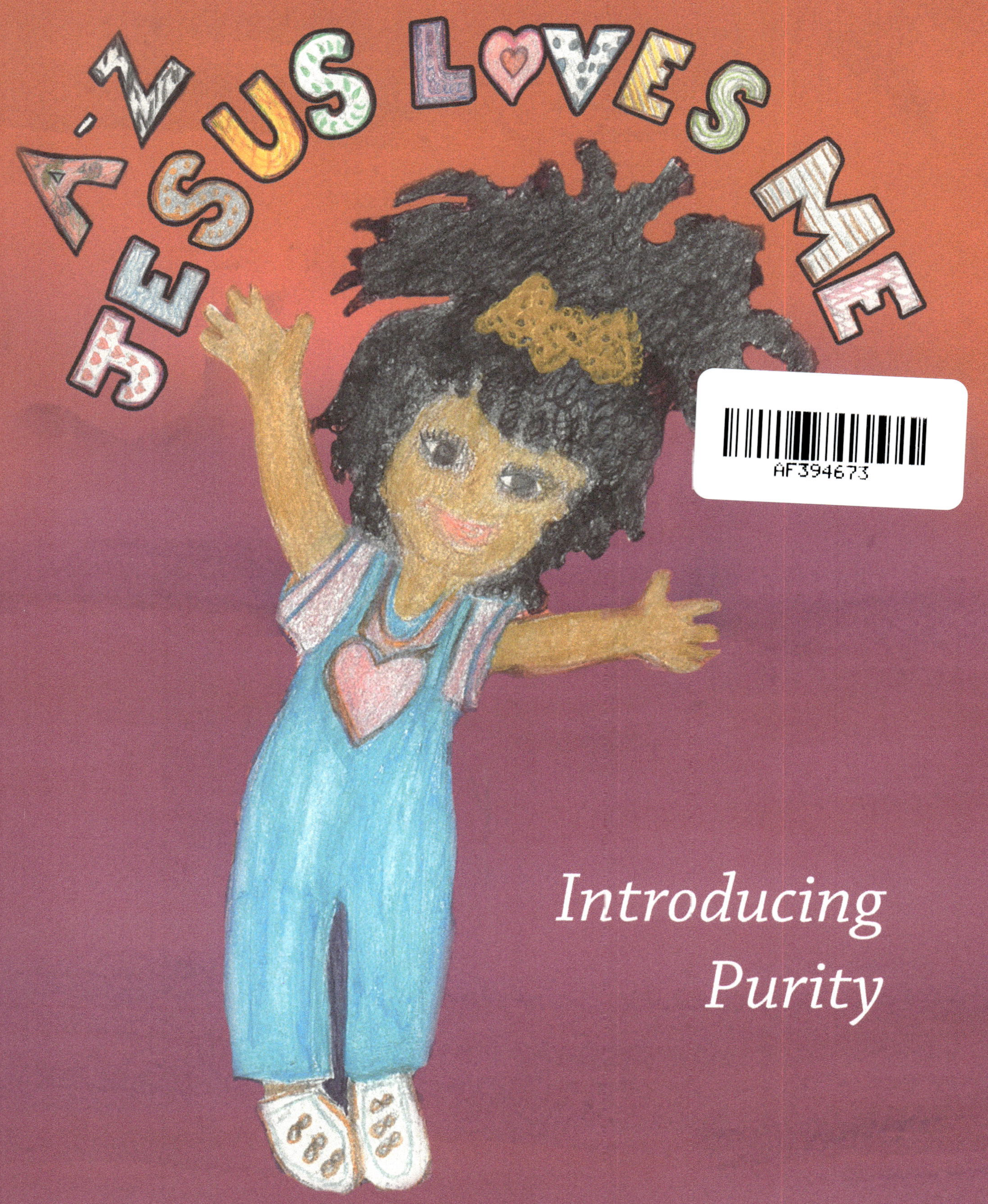

Introducing Purity

TEMOLYN *and* **RAEVYN**

A-Z
JESUS LO
JE
TEMOLYN a

Introducing
Purity

d RAEVYN

AuthorHouse™
1663 Liberty Drive
Bloomington, IN 47403
www.authorhouse.com
Phone: 1 (800) 839-8640

Because of the dynamic nature of the Internet, any web addresses or links contained in this book may have changed since publication and may no longer be valid. The views expressed in this work are solely those of the author and do not necessarily reflect the views of the publisher, and the publisher hereby disclaims any responsibility for them.

Any people depicted in stock imagery provided by Getty Images are models, and such images are being used for illustrative purposes only.
Certain stock imagery © Getty Images.

Scripture taken from the King James Version of the Bible.

Unless otherwise indicated, all scripture quotations are from The Holy Bible, English Standard Version® (ESV®). Copyright ©2001 by Crossway Bibles, a division of Good News Publishers. Used by permission. All rights reserved.

Scripture quotations marked NIV are taken from the Holy Bible, New International Version®. NIV®. Copyright © 1973, 1978, 1984 by International Bible Society. Used by permission of Zondervan. All rights reserved. [Biblica]

Scripture quotations marked NLT are taken from the Holy Bible, New Living Translation, copyright © 1996, 2004, 2007. Used by permission of Tyndale House Publishers, Inc. Carol Stream, Illinois 60188. All rights reserved. Website

This book is printed on acid-free paper.

ISBN: 978-1-7283-6772-9 (sc)
ISBN: 978-1-7283-6773-6 (hc)
ISBN: 978-1-7283-6771-2 (e)

Print information available on the last page.

Published by AuthorHouse 07/31/2020

authorHOUSE®

Dedication

For my daughters, Raelyn, Laela and children
everywhere, always know that Jesus loves you!

Raevyn

"Train up a child in the way he should go:
and when he is old, he will not depart from it."
Proverbs 22:6

For my generations, may God continue
to let us know He is everything.

Temolyn

"Tell your children about it, and let your children
tell their children, and their children the next generation."
Joel 1:3

A

God made everything yeah can't you see.
From the little ant to the great big tree.

D

E

B

C

Look over here, look over there,
He's everywhere!
A to Z Jesus loves me!

F

A
B
C
"Jesus said, Let the little children come to me, and do not hinder them, for the kingdom of heaven belongs to such as these." Matthew 19:14 NIV

Jesus Loves Me

A is for how **Awesome** is He
B **being** the person God wants me to be
C is for how He **came** and set me free

DEF
"I praise you because I am fearfully and wonderfully made: your works are wonderful, I know that full well." Psalm 139:14 NIV

He made me like himself

PICK
YOUR
OWN

D is for **distinct** unlike anyone else
E is for **each** and **every day** of good health
F is for **Father** who blesses us with wealth

G

God made everything yeah can't you see.
From the little ant to the great big tree.

J

K

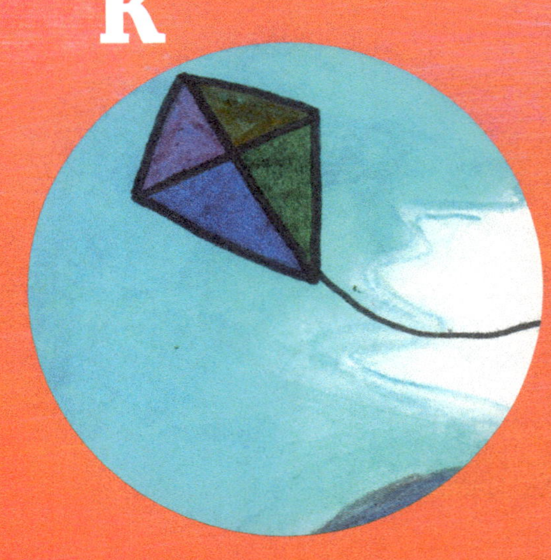

H

I

Look over here, look over there,
He's everywhere!
A to Z Jesus loves me!

L

GHI
"For you, Lord are the Most High
over all the earth; you are exalted
far above all gods." Psalm 97:9 NIV

He is the Most High
GOD is GOOD
HOLY BIBLE

LOVE

G is for **God** who we **glorify**
H is for **heaven** our **home** in the sky
I is for in His **image**, He made you and I

"Beloved, let us love one another, for love is of God; and everyone who loves is born of God, and knoweth God. He who does not love does not know God, for God is love."
1 John 4:7-8 KJV

# of His love I'll tell

J is for **Jesus** with Him all is well
K is for **King** He is the most noble
L is for **Lord** of His works I marvel

READ

M

God made everything yeah can't you see.
From the little ant to the great big tree.

P

N

O

Look over here, look over there,
He's everywhere!
A to Z Jesus loves me!

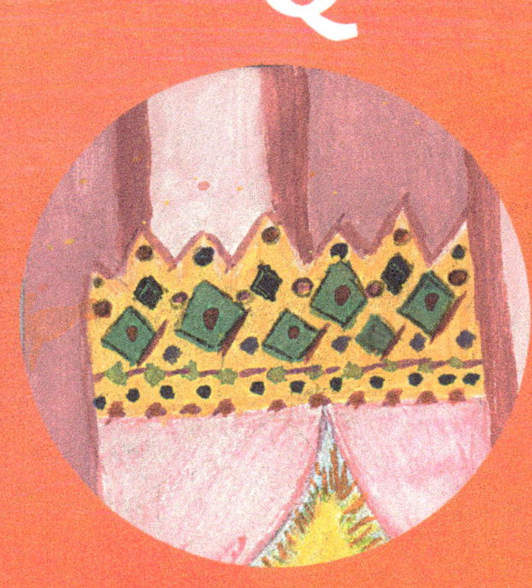

Q

R

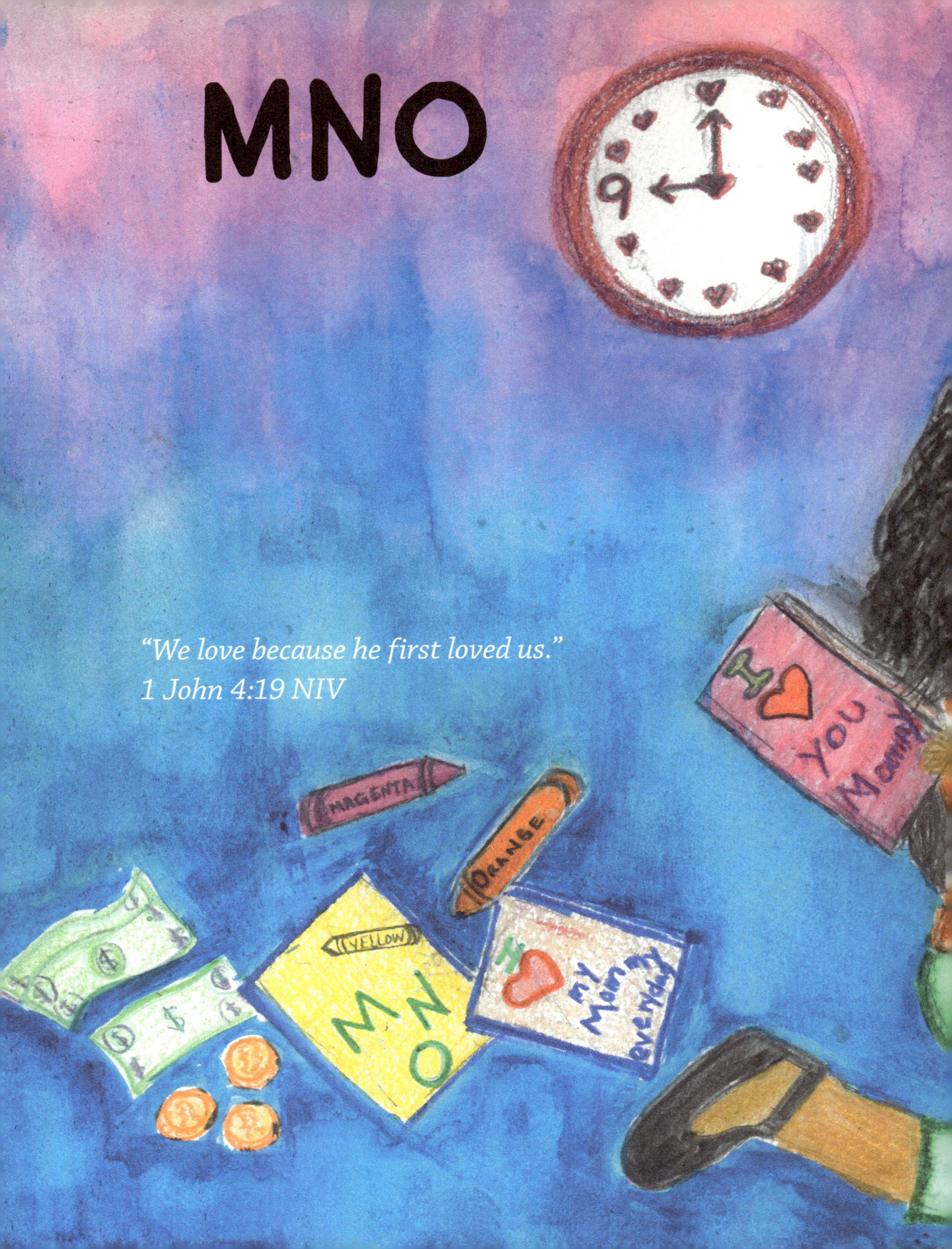

MNO
"We love because he first loved us."
1 John 4:19 NIV
MAGENTA
ORANGE
YELLOW
MNO
I ♥ YOU Mommy
♥ my Mom everyday

He loves
us so

M is for **mercies** today and tomorrow
N He will **never** give up or let us go
O is for **Ohh** Jesus loves us, this we know

P Q R
"Draw near to God
and He will draw
near to you."
James 4:8 ESV

PRAISE
Jesus is
never far

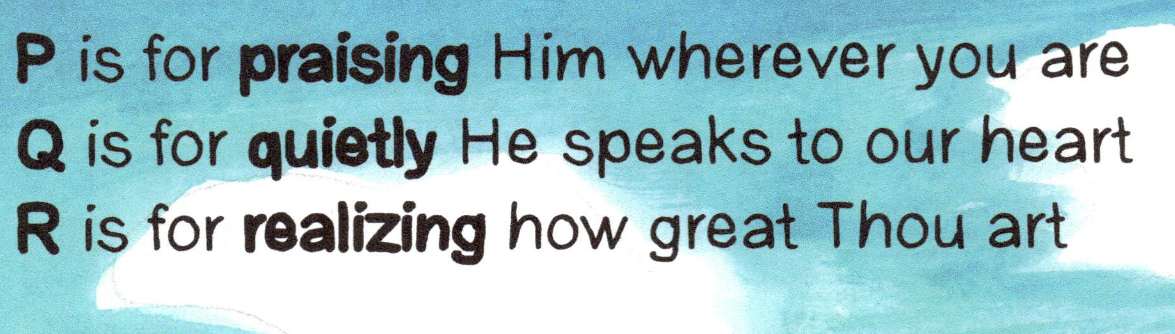

P is for **praising** Him wherever you are
Q is for **quietly** He speaks to our heart
R is for **realizing** how great Thou art

S

God made everything yeah can't you see.
From the little ant to the great big tree.

V

T

U

Look over here, look over there,
He's everywhere!
A to Z Jesus loves me!

W

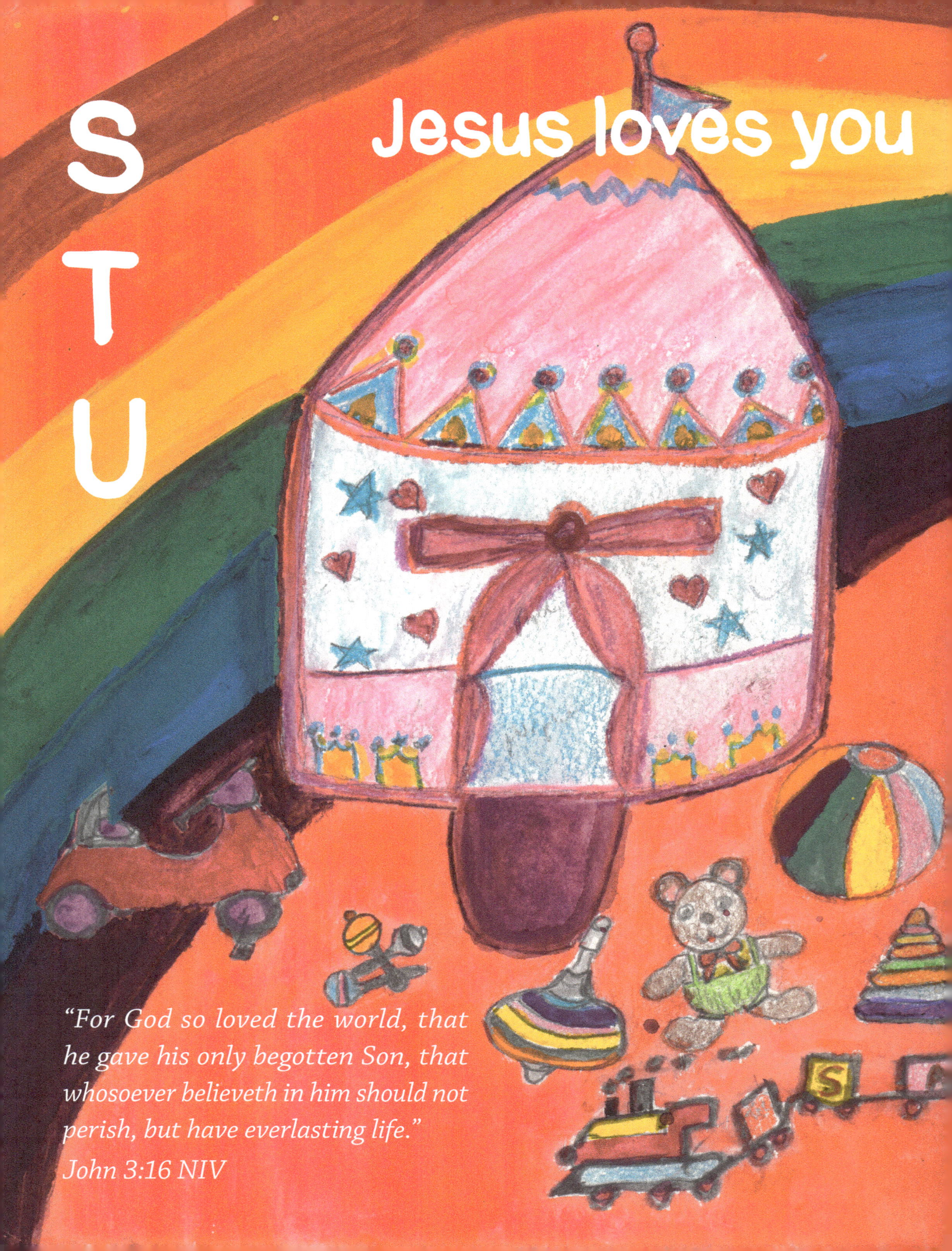

S
T
U
Jesus loves you
"For God so loved the world, that he gave his only begotten Son, that whosoever believeth in him should not perish, but have everlasting life."
John 3:16 NIV
S

S is for **Savior**. He gives us life anew
T is for being **thankful, trusting** and **true**
U is for the **unbelievable** works you do

V W
God's Word
is truth
"I have no greater joy than to hear that my
children walk in truth." 3 John 1:4 NIV

V He gives us victories and virtue
W wonderful God we worship You

X

God made everything yeah can't you see.
From the little ant to the great big tree.

Z

Y

Look over here, look over there,
He's everywhere!
A to Z Jesus loves me!

XYZ
ZERO

Jesus loves me

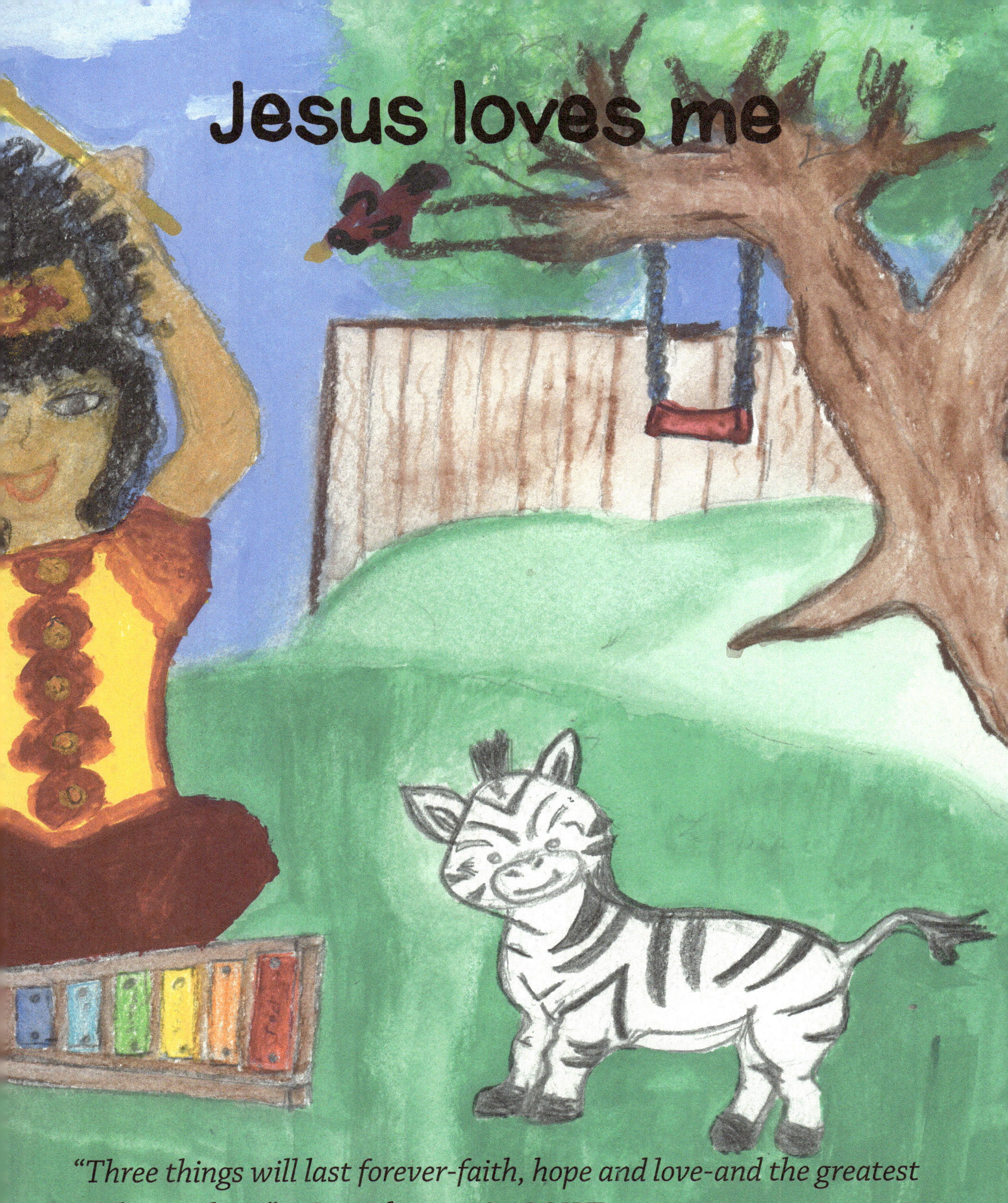

*"Three things will last forever-faith, hope and love-and the greatest of these is love."*1 Corinthians 13:13 NLT

X He blesses us e**X**ceedingly
Y is for **You** who made everything be
Z an ama**Z**ing God is He

God made everything yeah can't you see.
From the little ant to the great big tree.

Look over here, look over there,
He's everywhere!
A to Z Jesus loves me!